The nineteenth century was considered a golden age of wine—exemplified by improved production techniques, better bottle making and the spread of the corkscrew. But it was also at this time that the temperance and teetotalism movements reached their heights: societies for studying inebriation began to be set up. No wonder, given that many nineteenth- (and twentieth-) century British prime ministers were habitually drunk.

But Thomas Tylston Greg's loving address to the various kinds of wine was written not from a position of fear or of temperance, but from one of deep affection and intimate knowledge of the drinks he loved so much.

The books in "Found on the Shelves" have been chosen to give a fascinating insight into the treasures that can be found while browsing in The London Library. Now celebrating its 175th anniversary, with over seventeen miles of shelving and more than a million books, The London Library has become an unrivalled archive of the modes, manners and thoughts of each generation which has helped to form it.

From essays on sherry and claret to a passionate defence of early air travel, from advice on how best to navigate the Victorian dinner party to accounts of European adventures, they are as readable and relevant today as they were more than a century ago—even if wine cellars are nowadays considered slightly less necessary for one's dignity!

THROUGH A GLASS LIGHTLY

Confession of a Reluctant Water Drinker

The London Library

Pushkin Press

Pushkin Press
71–75 Shelton Street,
London WC2H 9JQ

Selection and editorial material © Pushkin Press and The London
Library 2016

Thomas Tylston Greg, *Through a Glass Lightly*. London: J.M. Dent
& Co., 1897

"In Confidence" by Charles Keene (1823–1891), published in *Punch;
or, The London Charivari*, May 10, 1884

First published by Pushkin Press in 2016

9 8 7 6 5 4 3 2 1

ISBN 978 1 782273 15 8

Set in Goudy Modern by Tetragon, London

Printed by CPI Group (UK) Ltd, Croydon, CR0 4YY

www.pushkinpress.com

THROUGH A GLASS LIGHTLY

BY THOMAS TYLSTON GREG, 1897

THOMAS TYLSTON GREG was born into the vastly wealthy Greg family, owners of Quarry Bank Mill, in 1858. Rather than going into the family business, he chose to work as a solicitor, and married the forty-five-year-old Mary Hope when he was thirty-seven. He was an art lover with a passion for fine wine, known for his "rugged vitality and ever-present sympathy". He died in 1920.

To my father
from whose generous cellars
has floated up
much of the inspiration
of the following essays
I dedicate
not inappropriately
this little book

Prefatory Note

My thanks are due to the Editor of the "Pall Mall Gazette" for permission to republish two of the following essays. The rest, with one exception, appeared in the "National Observer," and it is a matter of profound regret that, owing to the surcease of that paper, I can no longer ask permission of its former Editor to republish them. It would not be easy for me to repay Mr W. E. Henley the deep debt of gratitude I owe him for the literary encouragement which, in common with many others, I have always received at his hands.

T. T. G.

KENSINGTON, OCTOBER 1897.

PORT

"CLARET FOR BOYS" (methinks I hear the Great Doctor with superb finality), "Port for Men, and Brandy for Heroes." Probably he was right—he so often was right. But a change has come: at this present he would scarce endorse his judgment. Not with unquenchable thirst, and head and nerves immovable, do we drain off those brandies and waters on which our Benbows suffered and were strong. Men have been since Agamemnon, and men will be. The heroic is still attainable; but it has changed its environment, and to seek it in the *petit verre*, sipped as a digestive after the banquet's close, were a vain and idle thing. But Johnson speaks truth in the main; for to hack our retracing way through the impenetrable thicket of the years into that sweet and flowering meadowland of adolescence, where the wine was but an attribute of dessert, and it was among the dried cherries and the Elva plums that you looked for its essentials; to transport our big hulking bodies into that ineffable backward, when power was potentiality at best, and ignorance at worst was bliss; to do this, I say, is merely impossible. If Claret be for Boys, and I neither admit it nor deny, then is that cellar closed. But to be Men is for all of us; so for Men is Port. I had said it is the sole and only drink; though many excellent—comparatively excellent—folk there be that give the palm to ginger beer. And yet, on mature reflection, the earlier thought, quick-leaping and unpremeditated, was best. Yes; Port is the only drink. Drink, mind you: not nectar, as some would have you believe! Nectar is but a vague and shilly-shallying poetasterism, which can by no stretch of language be applied to the nobler stuff. For the gods, and Primitive Man in their image, drank only when they were athirst. They never sipped their liquor. Not theirs (poor devils!) to roll it round the tongue, to toss it playfully against the palate, to let it trickle exquisitely down a gullet of educated sensibility.

They quaffed it, they swilled it, they sluiced the drouth out of their systems with it. Nectar was mere stuff with a flow in it; a bulky flux which they drank from great bowls and tankards. They knew nought of palate; only that Nature abhors a vacuum. The state they ambitioned was at best a kind of convivial repletion. In the matter of liquor, the Olympians were co-mates and brothers in ignorance with the Teutons of the Dark Ages. These called their "bene bowse" Nectar, those others, Mead. And Mead, in truth, it was: sweet, clammy, cloying, over-rated Mead.

It is otherwise with Port. Only when the grosser cravings are appeased; when a ruined continent of beef has been toppled down the kitchen stairs; when the jellies and kickshaws are laid waste; when the crumbs are brushed away; when the fair stretch of napery has been whisked into space, and your glowing face beams back at you from the warm, rich, hospitable lustre of the mahogany; when silver reflects its reverted image, and the whole table is alive with light and gladness—only then does the Chief Priest bring on, in that splendid shrine, agleam with

11

an hundred facets, the drink for which Boys are inapt and Heroes unsuitable. In his baize-keeled cradle the giant magnum moves slowly with all the solemnity pertaining to a religious rite around the brilliant woodway; then tongues are loosened, and the joy of life runs high. It is great and good, this antique use of drinking after dinner. What boots it that *gourmets* like Sir Henry Thompson declare against it? 'Tis dying, if you will; but it dies hard as things British are wont. It has its enemies. The cigarette—a poor thing and any-body's own—makes advance all but impossible: also a fatal fashion would seek to cast the great liquor from us, and, ignorantly, would have us eschew our Port as a fiery and a heady creature, the sure and faithful ally of the Old Campaigner, Gout. Yet these same weaklings, still constrained by a custom they abhor, are found offering at the dinner's end the three fallen Graces—Port, Sherry, and Claret. Still the Triumvirate (for with wine there is no sex, only age and origin) goes its unhonoured round. For who greatly lusts after the cellars of moderate drinkers, men who too often buy at a venture? And especially is this

the case with Port: in whose quest they betake
them to their wine-merchant as one should go
to his doctor, with medicinal rather than purely
hospitable motives. Thus cometh in our midst the
Old Tawny, long in the wood, a renegade and trai-
tor, which hath imparted to dead timber that rare
and fragrant quality which should have exalted
a living palate. Of a brave look, but *sans* character, *sans* style, *sans* everything but liquidity,
who does not know the wretch, and, knowing
him, long for the days that were? In truth, the
modern tipple (it deserves no better word) is mis-
erably wanting in the great bulk and body and
splendour of the vintage wines. Ah, those wines!
Whence cometh the wonder of them? The pure
grape they are *not*: for they are garrisoned with
the mercenaries of other lands, they are stored
with the heroic afflatus, they are watered with
the Water of Life. Yes; the great Englishman was
right when he pronounced them the drink of
Men; and had he but laid down his liquor as he
laid down his law, there had been some mighty
drinking in Gough Square. Yet it is recorded of
him that he would drink twelve cups of tea at a

sitting, and barter the wealth of Oporto for the tailings of Bohea! Of such differences are our best and worthiest compact.

He is a true aristocrat, this Port of ours. He disappears into the mists of antiquity, but even thus you see the round and top of his royalty dim shining through the haze which is years. The living generation—republican in fibre, revolutionary in spirit, redolent of fusel and of fizz—recalls not the vintages coeval with Nelson, contemporary with the Duke. Waterloo Port is a tradition, indeed; for itself we know it not, nor are worthy to know. The "crowning mercy" of '32 (the Reform Bill) was followed by the blessed vintage of '34—*post hoc sed non propter hoc*; and it has been said with truth that the chief, if not the sole, effect for good of that middle-class Magna Charta was the building of the Reform Club; for here at least are cellars stored with the wine of wines, and thereof some of Mr Gladstone's starkest opposites counted it their especial privilege to drink. And thereafter Time hath marked his line of advance with halt after halt of noble vintages: even as our Royal Edward planted a cross at every resting-place of his Queen on her solemn march to Westminster. There is '47, matchless, incomparable, rare and precious, as the sea-otter; there is '51, honoured, as they say, though not drunk by the austere editor of *Truth*, which shows that in the radicalest of us lie the germs of nobility; there is '58, whose dry humour is appreciated by all them that love their Burton and their Lamb. And, there is '63; and thereby hangs a tale: for a reserve cuvée of him lay long unknown in the Reform Club cellars; and it had been there unto this day, had not a misguided Committee invited the Devonshire to sojourn for a while. There was a second Exodus of the Chosen People, as erst of their fathers under Pharaoh. And centuries of persecution were avenged in six weeks; and the face of '63 has vanished from the R.C. list.

Of '65, '70, '75, and '78 you shall easily judge for yourselves. Last, but not least, is the Port of Victoria's first Jubilee. That our Sovereign should rule an Empire over which the sun sets not is a trifle, an astronomical juggle, a common jingo yawp. The true secret of her strength lies here: that at least nine times in this glorious reign of hers, she could have filled the dungeoned cellars of Windsor with more illustrious prisoners than the Tudors; just as the secret of her weakness—if she have any—consists in that she didn't do it. Oh, the pity of it! If you may believe your society prints, she drinks nothing but whisky-and-water and a little dry champagne. Yet, at the last, her subjects and their descendants shall softly close their eyes, and drink in Jubilee Port the memory of her in whose honour it is named. So shall their loyalty stay unimpeached and unimpeachable. And yet it is hard to think of what might have been—and is not. One statue less, and—well, well! The Doctor was right; and Port is, after all, the drink of—not Boys, not Heroes, not even Empresses and Queens, but—Men.

CLARET

Those there are to whom it has ever seemed the gravest of misconceptions that a man cannot love two at once: that (so to speak) he cannot carry a change of raiment in his knapsack, when no climate in the world is so captious or so variable as that of the Land of Love. But I have never shirked the confession that, though full-blooded Lydia may sway my grosser affections, gentle Dorinda hath ever the softer place in my heart. Therefore, it is with no dread of a charge of inconsistency, "the foolish hobgoblin of little minds," that, while firmly avowing myself the leal bondman of Port, the master-wine, I would still go far out of my way to take the wages of that gentler sovereign of the senses, Claret. Between comparison and contrast is a great gulf, the one being odious and futile, the other obvious and of purpose. So in men's minds shall these two wines be still at strife for mastery, and none can dogmatically declare who is premier, and it shall remain a question of individual palate till the end. Also a man's mood shall set now this and now that in the foremost place. For if he would go down in a fiery-heated flood, oblivious of all save the glory of his submerging, by all means let him plunge into a sea of Port. He shall the quicker reach the shade, and once there, whether it be grape or gooseberry is all one. But there be times and times, and there lurks in all of us the longing to scale Olympus, and be lifted into the Muses' battle; and at such a pass, it is the hour of Hautbrion, the moment of Margaux, the instant of Latour and Larose. Pactolus himself flowed with no richer burden; better than grains of gold are borne in Larose's smooth-tongued flood, and whoso drinks of his "purple tide," from him the cares of the world go vanishing, vanishing, with a voluptuous and entrancing effect of delay. With Port we go down gloriously, but precipitately, into the couch of kings; we nestle into Luxury's lap; but we sleep on the instant. To a splendour of light succeeds an abysm of dark; there is no moment of twilight, no tutelary *crepusculum*, wherethrough to watch the fading glow we leave, and discern the gradations of the nearing dark. But Claret bears us ever up and up toward the light.

Liquid rejects its inherent properties: the stream mounts high and higher to the fount and source of things, even Aganippe's self. Skyward soar the fancies, airier grow the wits, the summit is in view, and man is worthy his privilege. With Port we lose the senses, with Claret we exchange them. The commonplace becomes romantic, the accountant precedes a poet. He has spurned the brute earth, and his hand has touched the shoulder of Pegasus himself. That he cannot mount is no fault of the charger that is ready to bear him heavenwards. Not even Claret is omnipotent.

It seems out of the nature of things that man should be drunken, as we use the term, on so admirable a liquor, and so it has ever appeared to me a mistake that Ripton Thompson should have been permitted to drown his five wits in Claret. Surely champagne had been meeter. But this Claret is ever being diluted with abuses, and it scarce surprises that a great man's name should be evermore associated with a coloured concoction which the unthinking persist in calling Gladstone Claret even unto this day. So is a lordly title dishonoured in the application. Yet that one, of whom it has sometimes been asserted that his promises are writ in water, should find his immortality traced in the nobler fluid affords matter for thought.

But to the name itself there clings a romance no politician nor any touting advertiser can wholly degrade or dispel. His father-grape is himself a true patrician, abiding in fair Châteaux, with ancient honey-sounding names and yet so poor withal that, if truth were told, the most of these holds are unfurnished and dismantled, and many are not in France at all, but (alas!) in Spain. The soil of his garden is of such magnificent sterility that any of less lineage would starve. Yet has he such a grace as, search God's most fruitful valleys as you may, you shall never find again; for it is the grace of gentle blood that is unadulterated with the prosperity of richness. What boots it that, flushed with the fat of Californian uplands, or bloated with the middle-class pride of Australian vineyards, these Colonial braggarts would seek to disinherit their brother of Bordeaux? They cannot do it; his title is indefeasible. So they come and go to the tune of "Tin-tara-boom-de-ay" on a very brazen band: which is, perhaps, as it should be. And while ever trying to persuade the world they are as good as he of Bordeaux, they do not call themselves by names that enthral the ear and capture the purse, but are grossly ticketed Port type, or Sherry type, or Claret type, as the case may be. Where, then, the wonder if men turn to hear of Château Pichon de Longueville, Château de Beycheville, Château Leoville? What flood but would seem glorious from illustrious founts like these? Yet is the method open to abuses. Such names are weavers of spells, and send you floating back to those happier ages when Scotland and France were more to each other than Scotland and England, and the link was this Claret; so that, as the years broadened into the later and bigger-drinking centuries, it came about that in Scotland there was good Claret and better Claret, but no bad Claret. They tell the same tale of Whiskey now: of Claret——not. Yet, though we may still find "Gladstone" flooding the cellars of Scots who should know better, there is a feeling in the air that traditions are not quickly broken, and that such Claret is still landed at the Port of Leith as the Port of London can never hope to acquire.

The world is growing bigger and bigger, and though the ranks of the Teetotaller are "swellin' wisibly," the God Dionysos still holds his cult, and the wine merchant looms large on the horizon. He comes on the wings of the circular, and clad in the raiment of hyperbole, flagrantly disregarding the adage that good wine needs no bush, and the pages of his catalogues are strewn with false and perjured epithets. So great are his eulogies of what he is pleased to call his "light Clarets," that for the real thing, if he have it, language falls too short for adoration. To begin with superlatives at the lowest rung of the ladder is to make sure of vertigo and a plunge into anti-climax from the top: so his "grand wines" remain in splendid isolation, whence their three figures alone convey a sense of excellence. Yet even here a man may be undone, and the Claret of his dreams remains an airy phantasm: for though he may find in a day, if his purse be long enough, a Port that is irreproachable, it demands a more arduous pilgrimage ere he come on an incomparable Claret.

SHERRY

It is not uncommon to hear of a poet that he is a poet's poet; of a musician, he is for musicians first and laymen after. So it is scarce matter for surprise to learn that a wine there is that is pre-eminently the wine merchant's wine. That this should be Sherry is all but inevitable; for he carries not his credentials with him like the rest, but trusteth chiefly to the praise and the recommendation of another, and that other the wine merchant aforesaid. And though it were too much to say of him that he has inspired a litera-ture, there has grown up around him a copious "derangement of epitaphs," with no little quaint learning; and let us say at once that, whatever his origin, he has grown manifestly, and flagrantly, *bourgeois*. As often as not, he is not Sherry, but Sherry-Wine: a most fiery, damnable, and discouraging beverage. In his working suit he tempers the ham sandwich to the shorn stockbroker, and divides the business day into meted periods; and thus far has his uses. His tastes are commercial, and he rarely enters the realm of fancy; for, though he is an emolument of laureates, it is doubtful if he ever inspired a stave of true poetry. The odd part about him is that he is inordinately ours, and is more at home by Thames' side than on the banks of the Guadalquiver. By travelling hitherward so oft and for so long a time, he has become more British than home-brewed October—and not much less than Burton's Bitter, or Dublin's Stout. And the chief factor in his adoption, his territorial sponsor, has been the wine merchant, of whom he has ever been the plaything and the wordy sport.

Mark this, and how thin the line that divides literature and commerce! And log-rolling is seen to be essential and evident in the profession of vintner as in the trade of author. In truth, his importance in the world of wines is as much due to the puff adulatory as are the stories of Mr— or the poems of Mr—, in the world of letters. For look you how this wine has been puffed and extolled! On him has been expended that wealth of superlative patter, for him has been invented that special jargon of exaggeration, whereby his vendors have given him a look of virtue, even though he have it not. And so, from being a mere appanage, a kind of spouse lawful of Plum Cake, this Sherry-White-Wine has attained to the dignity of an aboriginal, and upon him has been set the seal of legitimacy. Yet is he the most degenerate of bastards. His veins channel the mixed bloods of a dozen stocks. He is the very mulatto of wines, and art plays well-nigh as many freaks with his complexion as nature with her noblest creation; for he is now the very brownest of browns, and anon is stricken with a pallor that all but fetches him flush with the dominant race. At one time his odour is pervasive and insistent; at another his bouquet is so volatile that only the most curious observer may discern the essence. And if sometimes he should attain to royalty, it is the royalty of Mumbo Jumbo and Theebaw, not that of Victoria or the Hapsburgs. For his blood has gone wofully astray. The founder of his family lies embalmed in some splendid sarcophagus of Spain, same vinous vat of Xeres; and no man living, no, nor his grandfather neither, remembers when he was born—nor so much as when he was crowned. But his has been the royal privilege, that he should be the father of his people, or, at least, of a great many generations. *Divide et impera* has been the motto of his house, and the virtue and strength of him have been blended in many strains.

How, then, can we honour him in these innumerable descendants? Birth will out from time to time, but education and environment are potent factors in lineal deterioration. Haply, if we are lucky, we fall in with cadets of the direct line, bearing about them inalienable traces of their sovran origin; and these we lure into our own service at a recognised pay of some fifteen to twenty shillings a head (or bottle). But the great clan itself is so many thousands strong that its value is scarce as many pence per cork. For these needy rapscallions the wine merchant's office forms, as it were, a Labour Bureau, where they hang about till some one takes them on: or they flow over into the vaults of the Bodega, there to levy blackmail on the stomachs of public citizens, and tweak the noses of the *dilettanti*. Nevertheless, this Sherry is a force to be reckoned with; he is a monster of our creation, and we must treat him well or he will get the better of us, poor Frankensteins that we are. So, then, we cannot blame the wine merchant for writing the creature up, and allowing his imagination to get the better of his veracity or his professional zeal to top his individual integrity. For our part, when we read of "Magnificent Golden Sherry, thirty years in bottle, full, rich, without sweetness, with superb bottled flavour," we never think of questioning if such things be or no, but are filled with gratitude for so golden an opportunity. It is only five-and-forty shillings; and it were surely cheap at anything under a hundred! A still, small voice (with a strong Scots accent) whispers us to sample; salvation cometh not from the East or from the West, but from the North; and for this "Old Pale Oloroso Pale Sherry"—whatever whiff of romance the re-duplication of the epithet, the reiterated pallor, may have imparted, is now for ever flown. And if it were not, it were utterly dispelled by this further essay

in description: "A good, sound, clean wine, with
plenty of flavour and free from heat"; for that
label, "a good, sound wine," is even the most dam-
natory ever conferred. Yet is it meant to please;
and would seem to fulfil its destiny—for catalogues are innumerable as leaves in Vallom-brosa,
and in all lurks the pernicious phrase. Verily, these
Balaams of the wine trade set forth to bless, and
yet for all their efforts they end by placing a curse
upon their wares. The egg merchant is, we pre-
sume, the social inferior of the Vintner; yet what
a lesson the one may learn from the other! For,
consider the magnificent intensity, the superb
restraint, of this announcement:

New-laid eggs . . . . 2d. each
Fresh eggs . . . . 1½d. each
Eggs . . . . 1s. a doz.
Cooking eggs . . . . 6d. a doz.
Eggs for electioneering . . . 2s. 6d. a hundred
    purposes

Ever so much is said, and how few the words!
It is the padding of a volume in the pith of a

paragraph. On such lines should catalogues be built. Four epithets at most, and the whole kingdom is neatly and exhaustively differentiated. To the Man of Eggs, you, Man of Wine, and learn wisdom and the "value of reserve."

Spain's chivalry was laughed away these many years agone, but you cannot laugh away Spain's potent Sherries. They grin at you over the tops of multitudinous vats, and there is never an Englishman but knows the grimace. The wine (the Sherry Wine) is present wherever our language is spoken; its appearance with the soup is as regular as the tureen, and very near as indispensable; a dinner without it were second savagery and mere amorphousness. It is the soul of a cocktail and the body of bitters. You still can drink it in hours when to drink aught else would write you down a "nipper." No funeral is complete without it, and it is never absent from a wedding, where it affords a pleasant stimulus to the hired waiters. In good old-fashioned houses it is held the only refreshment. It is gifted with a peculiar capacity for penetration; and if we are troubled with livers, and things of that sort, it finds us out quicker than any other potable. However, it retains two privileges, one of which it shares with Madeira, but the other, poor thing though it be, is its own. It claims by prescriptive right the extraordinary epithet of "nutty," and—it serves for a whitewash!

CHAMPAGNE

It is in accordance with the eternal Unfitness of Things that Sparkling Champagne—that river on whose foaming stream, to the accompaniment of whose gallant laughter, two centuries of blades and Cyprians have floated bravely down into the gay backward abysm of Time—should have taken its rise in a Benedictine abbey. Yet in 1670, at Haut-Villers, one Dom Pérignon scored history with a thicker line than ever was drawn by William of Orange in 1688 of blessed memory. It took an Act of Settlement effectually and finally to abolish Divine Right; but in 1680 the dynasty of Still Champagne was quietly wiped out of being by a pacific friar. It perished perfect, consummate, unregretted—for the usurper proved himself omnipotent. The invincible Dom Pérignon, some ten years earlier, had lighted on a precious hoard beside which the Abbé Faria's was a trifle: for it was a case of incalculable milliards. And though the founder of a line is ever its greatest hero, so that Napoleon the Little is the natural complement of Napoleon the Great, this monk contrived to maintain the splendour of his order. He imparted his secret only when, in *articulo mortis*, he placed the crown on the head of Friar Philippe, his legitimate successor; who in his turn bequeathed it in 1765 to Brother André Lemaire. And this one reigned for thirty years, an enviable despot, and passed it down to his successor Dom Grossart. And he, having the Moets among his subjects, died with his secret big and undivulged, and the line and dynasty of Dom Pérignon was extinct. And none was greater than the Founder, who, arch-celibate though he was, yet made conjunctions happier far than all the rest of the clergy put together; for so consummate was his skill, and so exquisite his palate, that, being blind with years, he would taste you grapes from a score of vineyards, and decree that the wine of this one must be married to the wine of that; and his fame was great in the land, and the people would have his wine or none. And as the greatest mind is that which can adjust itself to the smallest details making for perfection, so this our benefactor, discarding the oil-steeped wisps of tow which till his time did vulgar service as stoppers, invented corks. So, too, he established the long, flute-shaped glass wherefrom to drink the elixir he had found, and wherein, like a true hedonist, he might watch the merry atoms frisk and dance like winter stars in running water.

It is also of the essence of a great discovery that it should come at the right moment, and this thing sparkled into being when the fortunes of France were on the ebb. So debilitated was the stomach of the Grand Monarque, that Fagon, his good physician, had to forbid him all but the oldest Burgundy, and that most villainously laced with water. But this Dom Pérignon—how bright a herald, how inspiring a companion for his dull and lonely Maintenon, aweary with his tiresome wails, his enfeebled autocracy, and soured by the falsehood of her true position! What wonder if she and all the bloods and the grand dames and the lesser ladies drank of it and were glad, while

Louis looked another way and sipped attenuated Burgundy? Here was enough, you would think, to console their France under those terrific visitations of Corporal John's; yet the influence has passed clean from the land of its nativity, the genius of the people it represented has been carried to other shores. It has pierced the fogs of Albion, and made us for the moment the compeers of those brighter spirits across the Channel whose image and superscription it bears.

> De ce vin frais l'écume pétillante,
> De nos Français est l'image brillante,

said Voltaire; yet he told but a half truth, after all, for his countrymen for the most part drink it at this present heavy and sweet to an accompaniment of *marrons glacés* and such-like cloying cates. Happily our own habit is different; and herein shines forth the ancient insular superiority. Scarce has the fish, bull-headed cod or blushing mullet, swum into our ken, ere the cork leaps forth with a cloop of joy, and straightway, as on the approach of spring, the sap stirs and the buds of speech burst into life, and talk, reluctant and hidebound no more, bursts into many-coloured bloom. No longer in middle-class houses is the wine doled out like drops of blood, as in those ugly parties which Original Walker satirised. At this, the tail-end of our century, it pours like melting snow down Soracte's sides, or spring torrents in the Acroceraunian hills. The dullard stands amazed at his own wit; and the professional talker-out moves not to envy; and the sorriest dog of us barks in rhapsodies and epigrams. No less than Port it carries the vintage glory with it; for do we not speak of that '74 Perrier-Jouet (now for ever laid to rest in pious gastronomic cells!) as of darling poet or statesman idolised in the Abbey by the stream of Thames? And the masterful Eighties, the fickle, fleeting, delicate-souled Eighty-Fours, the once speculative, broadly-promising but now fully-realised Eighty-Nines—do we not discuss them, even as the children of our loins? Wine does more than generate talk: it is talk itself; and do we not glory somewhat in their prices and value our dinners by those Princes of the Blood with whom we are privileged to fraternise? And our preferences—how exclusively our own, how cherished, how esteemed! How this one will swear by the buff label of that Widow Clicquot, who takes precedence, and the wall of all other widows, save Mrs Wadman alone! Think, too, of the liquid splendour of the Irroy name, the mouthful of majesty in Deutz and Geldermann's Gold Lack, the aristocratic flavour of Duc de Montebello, and the disappointment bred of too great an intimacy with that titled impostor! Then, too, the utter exclusiveness of Heidsieck's Dry Monopole, the merry lilt of Pommery and Greno, the boom of Bollinger! Are we not familiar with them all? They are intimates at the eventful moments of our lives! We have trysted with them at the Continental, and in marbled halls, when

> " 'Love me' sounded like a jest,
> Fit for yes or fit for no."

At the wedding breakfast (an extinct ceremony) they have prompted mouthings in honour of the ladies, and composed whole speeches to the health of the bride. They have even soothed the savage breast at those great and heavy dinners in Cromwell Road where Uncle Boanerges plays the gouty Elagabalus once a year. Only at funerals shall be missed the captive bubbles struggling, and rightly, to be free: though here the need of them is sorest, and you must perforce put up with Marsala, or, if a first class interment, with brown Sherry.

Truly it is a beverage of romance and laughter, this Champagne. In the lush green by Upper Thames, when summer shines on the glancing hair, the corks have broken forth and shot skywardly, singing the song of prodigality and abandonment. To look at life through this clear and golden medium was to cast seriousness to the winds. Clouds would fleet past the midday sun and darken for a brief spell the moon of night: but in these clear depths there was nothing of cloud, nothing of shadow; only, as should be, a heyday of laughter and romance. For, of all the transparencies this world can offer, none is so beautiful; none is so precious as that through which you behold the shining soul of a jest. And where else shall you look for, and more inevitably find it, than in this

Dom Pérignon? God rest the good monk's soul! And thou, "animula, blandula, vagula," sweet spirit of the present, born to pass here and now, in this narrow space of sun between the grisly past and the yet grislier future, rise up and still up from the source of things, even to this pleasant patch of surface! Actors love thee, and women; but for all that, rise, rise, rise ever; for once the beaded bubbles of ephemeral evanescence have winked their last, there is no deep so plummetless as that encircled by yon vacuous and reproachful glass.

BURGUNDY

If ever a wine ran a chance of being puffed to its damnation, that wine is Burgundy. For it is a favourite freak of the vintner to proclaim in his fly-sheets that he is now "selling at a ridiculously low figure a fine, full-bodied Burgundy, combining delicate aroma with grand *blood-making* properties." Now this is at worst to bring down one of the finest wines ever squeezed from grape to the level of a blood-mixture or a fruit-salt; and at best to hint darkly at what were better left to individual imagination, that these same vintners favour the cult of Aphrodite no less than that of Dionysos; and yet, after all, it would seem that they know their business, which is to vend at all hazards; and none is more keenly conscious that the specious flavour of an adjective may render palatable a whole dishful of unwholesome nouns.

The seductive epithet, indeed, is the licensed victualler's handiest weapon. For Saumur, unembellished by any qualifying epithet, we have scant affection, but to hear of it as " pale, dry, and *creaming*," and to see it foaming forth from the giant bottles on the posters at railway stations, is to create a thirst which must be quenched. And to lure us on to Burgundy by pronouncing it an Accretor of Blood is neither more nor less than to put a cheat upon us. For Burgundy, being the first red wine in the world, stands in need of no puffery. Not Claret itself can match it for richness and perfume. The aroma and bouquet as your vintner hath it, of a bottle of Volnay, to go no higher, will flood your chamber with the sweetness of an "unheard melody." Time was, some two hundred years since, when Burgundy and Champagne strove together for precedence. The question—*An vinum Remense Burgundico suavius et salubrius* was fought out in the schools between Physicians, grave and reverend, and Heads of Faculties.

Even as early as 1652 some fiery Burgundian had declared the wine of Beaune to be richer and wholesomer than any other, averring that Champagne predisposed to catarrh, gout, gravel, rheumatism, and such like disorders. Then rose up the men of Reims, and boasting the liquid purity, flavour and durability of the wine of their district, bravely asserted its unqualified superiority to all the wines of Burgundy. The senior physician of the Faculty of Medicine in Beaune defended his wine in a thesis which ran into five editions in less years; and thus the brave dispute was waged from generation to generation. Have we, then, no more to say of the wine to-day than that it possesses grand blood-making properties? Alas, we English hardly know it. For whoso would drink the true Burgundian elixir must seek the land of its adoption ere he shall light on perfection, since the grapes that yield it are the offspring of rare and favoured vineyards. True, there are good Burgundies in England, at a modest price even, which recall the prime growths at least in name; but it is a common trick to export the thinnest of wines under the style and title of the best. Thus, we can get Romanée Conti, which is the crowned king of all the Burgundies, at every restaurant. Of course we pay a high price for it, and yet it is well to remember that the vineyard which produces its incomparable grape is only six and a half acres in extent; that the wine is more highly prized in France and Flanders than in all the world beside; and that there still survive Frenchmen and Walloons of taste and purse. A word to the wise is enough, and lo, here are three!

As for Burgundy's heir-apparent, Chambertin, the favoured of Napoleon, he also is a native of an exiguous vineyard. Yet none in Paris enjoys a higher reputation, and it is idle to expect him this side of the Channel. Indeed, you must needs put up with Richebourg, Clos Vougeot, Nuits, Corton, Pommard, Volnay; even with Beaune and Macon. If these do nought beside, they may make you blood; and is not that, *teste* the vintner, the whole duty of Burgundy? Amongst white Burgundies it is hopeless, indeed, to find a blameless wine. Mont Rachet, if we could hit on the right quality, is fit for the symposia of the gods; but, alack, there be three kinds, and the value of the second is but half that of the first, and the third only a bare two-thirds the value of the second. If we would judge aright of the first red wine of France we must go to Brussels, to Dinant, to Charleroi, to Namur. Not on the banks of the Loire but of the Meuse dwell the folk who know what Burgundy is, what Burgundy means. Indeed, the inhabitants of the Ardennes care little enough for the choicer arts. It is not for them to collect enamels. Neither pottery nor pictures seduce them to extravagance. But religiously do they select and treasure their Burgundy, hiving it in cellars, the building and furnishing whereof have been the work of generations. No Walloon with pride of birth, of place, of purse, would ever sell his Burgundy at some Flemish Christie's. It was handed down to him by his father, and in due course, after the judicious disposal through sympathetic gullets of the older vintages, he in his turn will hand it down to his children. The great wine merchants whose enthusiasm is Burgundy are the Princes of the trade. Their dynasty is hereditary, and at Namur the grandson of Evrad, who supplied our grandsires, is still ready to take our own orders. At Brussels the name of Van Cutsem carries us still a step farther back. There for generations lies the wine in the great cellars of these greater men, each vintage awaiting its joyful resurrection. The cellars are deeply excavated as cellars should be, in the clay, or hollowed out of limestone rock. They preserve an even temperature of 50 degrees. Upon their doors the torrid sun may shine in vain. The whiffs of kitchen and the tremor of the streets are alike removed from the sacred shrine. Their bottles are yellow-black in colour, and from a cunning—begotten of long experience—are rough inside, differing herein from the bottles of Champagne which for a different reason are smooth on either surface. For it is well-nigh impossible to carry out the perfect maturing of Burgundy with a smooth-stomached bottle, for the deposit in the wines clings, as it should, to the roughened surface, and only the glory of the wine remains to drink, that would work its ruin blending not with it.

In the autumn following the vintage, the great Burgundies, which, in the hopes of men, already eclipse the ancestral vintages, pour into Charleroi and Namur. One by one the great years—1811, '34, '37, '39, '40, '42, '44, '46,

'48, and '65—have toppled off their shelves and live only in the memories of amateurs. Even now the Flemings are waiting with tiptoe expectation the development of 1889, of which it has been rumoured that none other save 1811 will surpass it. Yearly the value grows, and yearly more splendid and glorious the well-earned increment. The wine is bottled at the end of fifteen weeks, and some would say that it has passed its prime when sixteen years are told, which opinion prevails not in Wallonia. Your cunning wine merchant never clarifies his wine, and never delays his bottling beyond the appointed time. Also, he corks the bottles with the nicety of a worker in mosaics. Strange it is that the best Burgundy should find its way from the land of its nativity to Belgium, the land of its adoption; yet it is a notable and pleasant fact that a wayfaring man in the Ardennes may light on a bottle of wine of such a quality that he might search all England through with Fortunatus' purse and not meet withal. The best Bordeaux leaves not Bordeaux, but no one would go to the Bourgogne to drink its treasures.

The dispute which raged between Burgundy and Champagne in the seventeenth and eighteenth centuries could scarce be revived to-day. The partisans of Champagne would win by sheer force of numbers. Where two things are almost equally meritorious it were well to leave each alone, or swallow them in equal quantities. Horace praised Massic and Falernian, preferring this to-day, that to-morrow. For ourselves, we agree with a famous Canon of Reims who observed that "in the wine of Burgundy there is more strength and vigour; if it does not play with its man so much, it over-throws him more suddenly, as did Demosthenes. The wine of Champagne is subtler and more delicate; it amuses more and for a longer time, but in the end it does not produce less effect. Such was the result of Cicero's oratory." And the true amateur of the bin had rather have one bottle of either wine than the collected works of both orators.

MADEIRA

Let there be no mistake: we were wholly cognisant that Spring—revivifying Spring—was in the air. Nature was in the ascendant; and for Art—why, let her go hang! The world at such a moment as this bade us rejoice, and would not recognise the cloud upon our own brow. And yet the essence of storm and stress was there, irrepressible and irresistible; for though fogs were gone and east winds barely here, we knew that with Candlemas came the great annual sacrifice, the great refusal, to wit, the closing down until November next of the great bin of peerless Madeira—bottled, oh! ever so many years before the Consulship of Plancus and the like of him. For the romance of war is still in its blood, the war of North and South, the War of Secession, when a glamour hung over Charleston as a halo.

For old Jarrow of Manchester bought and fitted out a steamer at his own charges, as a gentleman should, and freighted it with arms and ammunition, forage and provant, and all things dear and precious to a beleaguered city. And for this latter end he sought help and equipment, among others, from our own progenitor, who, God bless him! stayed neither hand nor purse. And so this bark of good omen steamed bravely over the Mersey Bar, and as to what perils she ran through and what success achieved, are they not written in the ledgers of Jarrow and his compeers? But she emerged from Charleston Harbour unscathed and choked to the throat with her return cargo of cotton, and *longo tamen intervallo*, once again passed over the Mersey Bar, which ceased for sheer joy from moaning and groaning as was its wont. And Jarrow divided the profits, *pro ratâ*, with those who had helped him. And lo! at this time there came into the cellars or bonded warehouses of Liverpool a noble consignment of Madeira, so old that even then the memory of man ran not to the contrary, and the price went fairly over the three ciphers. And out of his Charleston overflowings,

the progenitor, wise father as he was, and knowing his own sons (then unborn) gave out the mere
dross of metallic gold, and took into his cellar
the Lord knows how many dozen of a gold that
had no equal; dark red, rich, beautiful sparkling
gold. These he placed in a great cradle in a little
room hard by and near to the genial warmth of his
kitchen fire, and then he bade the youngest of his
hirelings swing it night and day with a ceaseless,
tireless motion; and so with this warm and gentle
movement did he in his fervent imagination and
young heart contrive to give his beautiful peerless
wine a sea voyage to the East Indies, in his days
considered an essential part of an incomparable
Madeira's education.

And now, grown old and practical, with his
ardent imagination shrunken in the light of base
and common day, he has transferred the wine from
the cradle to its nursery in the solid sandstone.
And yearly from Michaelmas to Candlemas do
we his sons supplicate and partake of his bounty;
and now, alas! Candlemas comes and passes. And
so it comes about that Spring has no joys for me as
it has for others, and I hear the throstle's liquid

warble and the blackbird's piping with a mute indifference, for throstle and blackbird, thanks to God, reproduce themselves each year, but this Madeira is the last of his race, splendidly sterile and icily null, and already we seem to detect in the blood of him the faint suspicion of tartness, which tells us that the end is nigh. The bloom of age is passing away; he is already gliding into his second childhood, the end of which is death. And we fear, we brothers who mourn him together, that he should be drunk regardless of seasons. But for all that he is not a companion to dally with when the white chestnut blossoms are simulating snowflakes at Hampton Court, or the plash of Thames' waves is straining this way and that the reeds and irises on the bank.

Rather, this venerable fellow is the companion of the advanced Sybarite. He is a product of extreme artificiality; he has nothing in common with nature. Moreover, he induces, so his enemies assert, the fell Podagra or gout. But his colour! his bouquet! his flavour! Why, with all the faults lying at the back of him, do not these virtues of his throw all other wines into the shades of discredited liquids? He is so rare, so select, so refined. Few there be who can ever meet him face to face. He is filled with curious and quaint learning, and he has picked up in the common rooms of Oxford colleges a knowledge of mixed oaths and the now dead languages. He appears at fitful intervals at the tables of men who have heavy and loaded clarets, and ports that are of little good save to administer to the dying poor to accelerate their end. Now the reason of this is not far to seek. He is such a mysterious fellow that he has hobnobbed with a man's ancestors, and has taken up an abode in their cellars, and comes down to this ignorant generation by an accident of bequest or intestacy, and these modern heirs bring him out with a sort of mixed pride and diffidence, offering him as some old wine which "my grandfather" was sometime the possessor of; and few take him at a venture, lest, haply, he should pinch up their toes, and bring into their knuckle-joints those mysterious and painful globosities which are called chalkstones.

There is, indeed, a fashion to decry the wine, and he has suffered much from blight, and the roguishness of vintners; for when the demand in former years ran high, these sorry rascals substituted for the real Simon Pure low-priced fluids liable to turn acid, and so did he fall into disrepute. Also the First Gentleman in Europe in the early decades of this century, by cultivating and disseminating a preference for sherry, did much to put the nose of our glorious Madeira out of joint; for men are, alas! too apt to forget the glory of this Madeira and wholly to ignore his royal descent. It is a far cry to 1421, when Prince Henry colonised Madeira, the woody island, with grape stocks from Candia, and to this day the romance and joy lingers about these island vineyards. For the vines are planted upon lines of trellis-work in front of the houses, and the branches are deftly led over the tops, and the sun rays fall down and beat upon them horizontally, so that beneath is an arbour of shady and green coolness. And in other parts of the island they are trained up the wild chestnut trees, and themselves, as true children of freedom, acquire a vagabond and roving character. And again on the slopes, in full blaze and glare of the sun, do men grow the celebrated Malmsey, and the grapes whence proceed this notorious wine must needs be over-ripe and all but shrivelled, so that the juice expressed therefrom may be of an exceeding fragrance and superabundant richness. The highest quality Malmsey, with a proper sense of remoteness and insolent aristocracy, comes, or came, from a small avalanche of tufa lying at the foot of a cliff all but inaccessible. And one small farm only grows the wine which the Royal House of Portugal was wont to keep for its own exclusive use. And cousin-german to the Malmsey, through the collateral line, is the Sercial, descended from the grape which in other lands nearer home produced Hock; the wine of the Affinities.

So, do what we will, we cannot but doff our hats to this wine of ours, for we stand—in his presence—in the presence of royalty. And he has this endearing quality about him, that he and Time are such good friends and understand one another so well that age becomes him and is his charm, when with us poor men and women only too often youth is the one possession we are born with, which we have squandered ere we knew that it was worth anything. Now Madeira in his youth is harsh and austere, he has a pungent tongue, and speaks with bitterness; but age cometh over him, and, like a tender schoolmaster or parent, leads him gently along, and his tart sayings are metamorphosed into genial wit and a happy softness of utterance. His rough corners are rubbed off. The march of Time can do nothing against him, only to mellow and soften him and make us love him. Indeed, one can hardly be said to be on speaking terms with him unless we have him lurking in the wood these eight or ten years, and afterwards have completed his education and softened the acidities of his young temper in bottle for at least twice that period. Only after the lapse of several generations he falls into his second childhood, when he should be drunk and no more said. The ignorant bring him out with port and claret and sherry, and would have him play an insignificant fourth to the great triumvirate; but in reality he should come forth alone, he should sparkle and gleam in his flashing tower of old English glass. Alone and unaccompanied he should disappear slowly and with method down the throats of those who love him, conferring some essence of his own greatness upon them; for, great as he is in all other particulars, he has, above all, the indescribable qualities—style and distinction.

"IN CONFIDENCE"

Dining Room, Apelles Club

DINER: "Thomson, do the members ask for this wine?"
HEAD WAITER *(sotto voce)*: "Not twice, Sir!"

CELLARS

Not to have a cellar is derogatory to the dignity of man. Yet it is notable that, while every petty clerk or budding draper clamours for a bathroom, not one in a thousand will insist upon his wine vault; and so it comes to pass that Jerry the master-builder squeezes a new-style tepidarium into every one of his vulgar thirty-pounders, and the million which would be clean, but *is not*, flocks to wash therein. Yet is a hole under the stairs, or the divided honour of the larder held good enough depositing ground for the counterfeit presentments which—with the Lower Upper-Middles—do duty for Château Margaux and Sandeman's vintage ports. Apart from sentiment, which should hallow the Cellar no less than the boudoir, these people ignore the absolute necessity for a fit and proper wine place; and they are not a few who, like the sometime student of Gray's Inn, keep their wine under their beds (with the subtle plea that so it will be drunk the faster), or imitate that undergraduate who entertained a cask of beer by his bedside in case he might wake o' nights and feel athirst. But of such men we can seldom look for good wine; so it were idle to expect they should be duly considered in this matter, though there be few wines, and they the headiest, that can endure indifferent cellarage. Not even the perfect affinity which is the attribute of Hock, nor the brandied sinews of Port, can prevent their owners from being lamentably undone; while as for your delicate French wines, their portion is ruin, and the red precedes the white on the road to ruin. It is not every one, and least of all a Londoner or town man, who can scoop him a cellar under the living rock, which is the true matrix for the development of good wine; but you will find no finer hold than that which lies deep, some forty to fifty feet, as the soil allows, without excess of moisture, nor with any opening save one to the north alone. In populous cities pent, the least you should insist on is a chamber in stone or brick, contrived at such a depth as will secure an even temperature all the year round. Let it not be subject to the fickleness of the outer air; for in truth nor rain, nor drought, nor heat, nor cold, nor temporal things, nor things celestial, should vex the contents of your storied urns. If so be that you can have double doors, see to it that they are there, this one some four feet behind that other; so that the outer being closed ere the inner be set wide, one equal temperature of fifty degrees may be achieved, week in week out, throughout the ages. It is the habit of man to curse his wine merchant for sending another wine than that he sampled: yet it is very often not his wine merchant but his cellarage that has played the knave, and has given him the worse end of a bargain.

It is not less than marvellous that a good glass of wine is ever ours in town, for the urban cellar is not often ventilated, so that foul air and rank mists still penetrate through cracks and fissures in the brickwork. We can keep our neighbour out of our dining-room, but we cannot barricade our cellars against his atmosphere. These, for the most part, are run out beneath the street; the neverending flow of traffic keeps up a perpetual perturbation over our stacks of bottles, and, as over the engaging Williams, "drives for ever the uproar of unresting London," so that our wine, being never utterly reposed, is never wholly clarified. Moreover, unless our walls and our floors be damp enough, our corks will grow thin, and the wood of darling vat or cherished cask contract and gape; and the essence, the *animula*, within escapes; and the New Humourist is there to talk of whines from the wood. On the other hand, an excess of moisture breedeth mildew, which warps for wrong and rottenness the all-too susceptible cork. Thrice happy he, in truth, who can keep two cellars (as who should say a twin orchid house), the cool one for his more delicate exotics, his clarets, and his dry champagnes, the other for his more luxuriant growths, his *vins de liqueur*, his madeiras, sherries, ports! In this second chamber he may clap on an extra ten degrees and no harm done. For it must ever be borne in mind that wine is no mere fluid, but is informed with sensitiveness and has a most incomparable soul.

There should not be so much as a keyhole for the random gust of sewer gas; no squalid waft of cabbage water should ever whiff it to these secret shrines. In well-regulated houses, even the beer cellar is kept distinct from the palace of the grape; for it is a law of conduct with the true drinker that you shall not vulgarise your wines by so much as suffering them to neighbour with the baser potables. *Procul, O procul!* Hence, far hence, let beer and stout and cider and such hobnailed minor prophets be removed!

And, then, the bins and the mode of storage—what colossal opportunities are here for error! The shelves should be of stone or of brick, but of wood—never! No thickness of lime can wholly whitewash wood: no fermentable material, no acid, no liquor in a state of acetous agitation may enter the cellars of the blest. Above all, you shall flee from the spell of sawdust, the guide, philosopher, and friend of idiot butlers and 'prentice householders. For sawdust, if you only leave it long enough, breeds the creeping thing, and in decay it generates a gas no wine of delicate parts may breathe and live. Laths of wood, or, still better, slips of earthenware or terra cotta, alone should keep the crystal palaces apart; or you may imbed your happiness in quartz sand well washed in fresh water, in which wise you shall escape the outer darkness and enter upon the kingdom of light. Also remember that "A wine-cellar too hot or cold Murders wine before 'tis old"; and be your own cellarman.

A waitress, being a woman, cares nothing about wine and knows less. A butler either cares about wine, or does not. If he does, he drinks it; if he does not he gives it away. And let your cellar be a pattern of neatness, so that yourself can descend thereunto with pleasure, and conduct your friend with pride. Let it not be littered with the straw wigwams which protected the bottles ere yet you drew them into your own ensheltering pale. Remove those garish papers of primrose yellow and cold hard magenta which shrouded the taper elegance of your Hocks, or the mighty bulks of the giant guardsmen of Champagne, and drill their wearers with precision; for henceforth they are to be your Yeomen of the Guard, and not one of them but will quicken you with some bright jest or troll you off some score of merry songs. A brave tenant is worth a noble home; see you that he gets it. Let all be in order and in place: as in the heaven above, so in the earth beneath. There is none to dispute that all wines have a body, these Titanic and huge, those of more lissome build. Whatever their physical constitution, yours be it to maintain the existence of the soul and the imagination in them. You will find that though there be many dreams in a flagon of Burgundy, they are not of the stuff that common dreams are made on, and that you can interpret them or let them slip past you into thin air, according as you house your liquor well or ill. Place it in squalid tenements and among bare surroundings, and it will speak squalor and breathe base thoughts and low ideas. But place it in the palace that is its due, and the world shall find that when you go down into the bowels of the parish for a bottle, you bring up far more than a mere quantum of drink.

For the rest, let one simple rule prevail. Avoid the advertising vintner as you would the Devil, and hie you only to that fine, old, crusted, long-matured variety—known as the Old-Fashioned Wine Merchant. *He* will look after the buyer: it is for the buyer to look after the cellar. This reads like a verbal jest, no doubt; but it is a profound truth.

GLASSES

There is no action save upon a balance of considerations, and there can be no right drinking save upon a most scrupulous discrimination in the matter of glasses. For right drinking, being as it were a tourney of palatal sensations, is largely dependent upon its accessories, and the most important of these is the vehicle by whose means the tourney is accomplished.

Now, of glasses there be three kinds: the tinted or coloured, the plain, and that which is known generally as cut; and there be some wines that will shine with all, there be some that pair well with two, others there be that will mate with one alone. And first there is the bastard Sherry, that *filius nullius*, yet boon companion of all. Him sprung from unknown and unpedigreed parents, yet none the less apt to form a line of his own, you shall drink indifferently from glasses plain and glasses cut. His amber complexion sparkles and dazzles through the myriad facets of the one sort: so let the sport he makes the eye be held to compensate for any trifling deterioration of palate. But for all that, he flows the kindliest from a plain, clear glass, conical-shaped, lipped over at the rim, so that his oleaginous and flavorous qualities may linger a little on the lips ere he leave his temporary haven for a more blessed embarkation. And this, too, be it said, though the reverted apex is a source of pain and tribulation to housewives and to conscientious butlers, for no finger will stretch to its nethermost deeps, and nothing short of a slate-pencil wrapped in a dishcloth will ever clean its uttermost confines. For Hock, that fount of the affinities, no glass of English disposition fits him; and you must seek his true vehicle in those regions which of old time bounded Gaul and Germania, for neither in colour nor in shape shall you easily match them. But see that the stems of them be hollow and broad, and take heed that the hue of them be amber as in harmony with the genial creature they enclose, let the amateurs of green asseverate never so wisely, for thus do you impart the right ambrosial tinge. The clients of Ter Borch, Metsu, Hals, even Teniers in his gentler moods, inclined to a long and pointed figure; but it was a concession to pictorial effect, the stumpier vessels lending themselves less readily to the characteristics of a set of drinkers whose conviviality is roysterous in effect and type. The benignant quality of Hock is scarce suited to riotousness—appears expressed, indeed, for the sole delight of a leisurely and cultured palate. But this is mere opinion, and on this theme a difference is possible, and may be held with honour. At the next stage it is not.

With the Champagne man has become vainglorious: he is clamorous for a sign of the thing's own character, for the frolic vapours of him have extended to his accessories. Now, in the matter of his vehicle, it is hard if you do not find his adventitious vulgarity somewhat accentuated. And, most of all, the right drinker frets and chafes at the Champagne glasses of old-world hotels and private houses—the wide-throated, the over-proportioned—wherein the beaded bubbles waste themselves into thin air or ever his time for them is come. In drinking therefrom he may recall, perchance, some catchings of the breath, the advance-guard of that arch-enemy, the Hiccough. He resents that extreme circumspection which is needed ere he drink: for a man should think only of that which he drinketh, and not whether or no he will be able to swallow without bearing testimony to the indignant ear. Often, too, the stems of this species are hollow: to the end, their vendors tell you, that, being filled, they may sparkle and bubble like an Iceland geyser; and this the right drinker may not behold without suspecting that the dust has gathered there since the last using. Now, it is known that atoms of bread-crumb and all sorts and conditions of alien matter cause a spurious effervescence; but he holds that virtue all too dear at the price. On the whole, the thoughtful have ceased to expect the creature himself wholly perfected either in his integrity or in his proper continent at the hands of your private householder; since he will neither pay for the one nor shed his infernal prejudice regarding the other. No; for this they must turn them to the restaurant (or feeding-shop), or go unsatisfied. And yet the points of a Champagne glass are neither extensive nor peculiar. It should be so thin that it clings to the lips as a membranous transparency—a bubble divided in twain, and floating on the wings of the wind. It should be wider in the middle than at any other point; should taper thereto from the bottom, or therefrom to the top—so that the soul of the wine comes concentrated into the mouth of its high priest. To be utterly avoided is the narrow hollow stem, which habours dirt or—what is as bad—inclines to the suspicion of dirt. Absolutely to be shunned is the flat superficies, for that, for reasons already insinuated, it prevents that first long, liberal draught which stamps the dinner a success.

Concerning Port and Claret there is less to be urged. The last has suffered much at the hands of the so-called Aesthetic; for it is a crying insult that he should be drunk out of opalescent and of art-green contrivances, unearthly as to their shapes; as it is that he should be degraded to the horrible magenta globosities you find at refreshment-rooms and cheap hotels. For he is a colour to himself, and should only be savoured from pure white glass of wafer thinness, light as the fancy he inspires, large as befits the greatness of his soul, transparent so that his "purple tide" may ebb and flow in full vision. Now these points are for the most part recognised, so that you find him more aptly presented than any of his race. As for Port, so great is his predominancy that he would hardly be gainsaid, though you should take him out of pewter. You may buy his glasses by the pound-weight an' you will; but even Port responds to warmth and thinness; and for the shape it matters little. Also his affable genius still lends itself to cut-glass and diamond points, wherein you may behold him sparkling and dancing at you in the full strength of his unutterable imperiousness.

BUTLERS

The institution of Butlerdom is more British than Magna Charta, more emblematical of Britain's social slavery than trial by jury. And in our search after precedent we adduce with no little satisfaction the authority of Holy Writ. Indeed, it is hard to bring forward a stronger proof of the inspired character of the Old Testament than the subtle, albeit indisputably right, discrimination of that Pharaoh who lifted up the head of his Chief Butler and restored him, the temporarily deposed, unto his Chief Butlership, yet hanged on a high tree that overrated official, the Chief Baker. For it is difficult to picture the use in the scale of creation of a chief baker, a superintendent of concocted flours, a viceroy of crust and crumb. Bread, corn stuffs, farinaceous medleys, are but incidents of life; the pulse of it beats in ruby depths, or bubbles in amber fountains. How, then, shall a baker, be he chief or dependent, suffer other exaltation than a halter's?

Yet must it be conceded that opportunity, the Parent of Crime, is more exclusively the Butler's prerogative than that of any other living man. By what process it is hard to say; but he has acquired a subterranean Headship, a cellared monarchy, from which it will need a bloody revolution to depose him. He is the despot of the servants' hall, and the Plain Cook alone among women is held worthy to mate with him. His civil list exceeds that of the other Kings of Flunkeydom, and not only does he hold the gorgeous pantry in fee, but he has a reversion also to the best public-house in his parish. If he vacates the service of some Duke or great man, he becomes the long lease holder of a "Marquis of Granby," and acquires an importance and a rotundity of barrel worthy his high office. But though he is the emblem of British respectability, so that no house can ever hope to attain a mansional dignity without him, he is full of imperfections, and not seldom is wholly unworthy of the great price he brings. For his wages exceed the income of the inferior clergy, and his beer-money would float a fleet of nondescript writing "chaps" and literary "gents." His first duty is to give the cup into his Pharaoh's hands, his next to see that it be full and brimming, and his third to keep it shining and bright as the sheen on a summer sea. "As Argus had a hundred eyes for his sight, he should also have (like Briareus) a hundred hands wherewith to fill us wine indefatigably." He should have the soul of a *bon vivant* and the restraint of a Joseph. He should have the words of the old drinking song graven on his heart, or, at least, writ large in his pantry:—

> Remplis ton verre vuide,
> Vuide ton verre plein.
> Je ne puis souffrir dans ta main,
> Un verre ni vuide ni plein.

He should have a large sympathy with thirst; the void that nature and art alike abhor, he should ever be ready to fill; and if he cracks a bottle of your best Burgundy with your friend's "man," it may well be pardoned him, so that he sees you suffer no worse a fate. He should thieve in the grand style, and never condescend to take the heart out of a flask and fill the eviscerated shell with water; he should know that a bottle is of the aristocracy, and should ever treat it like a gentleman. What blow so hard to bear as the knowledge, years after you have sacked your incomparable butler for intemperance, that he had drunk three and a half dozen of your '47 port, and filled the bottles with the pure lymph in which you condescend to wash, but never debase yourself by drinking?

For ourselves, we scorn to set a watch upon our Lord High Keeper of the Vintages: we would as soon suspect one of Her Majesty's Judges of taking a bribe as imagine a dishonesty in our butler. There are men who keep cellar books, earmarking every bottle of every bin, so that at a glance they can see how much remains of that '75 Lafitte, and how many bottles of the '74 Pommery are still for self and friends; but we would put our butler on his honour, and inculcate him with the pride of cellarage, and the artistry of drinking. It may be that we err on the side of credulity, but while we remain in ignorance, we live in bliss. We have endured much at the hands of inexperienced waiters, for the name of butler predicates perfection; we have sat gloomily at dinner looking alternately at the empty glass, and the sable statue who alone could fill, standing in mute, passionless idiocy at the back of his master's chair, and we have debased ourselves by an appeal to him for potatoes, not from a craving for those starchy globules, but from an irresistible longing to whisper into his ear, and demonstrate the all-too-patent vacuity beside us. These men deserve and receive no compensatory vail. They stand, impotent expectants as they are, at the door on the day of parting; they have unpacked no portmanteau nor laid out any shirts; they have let one go night after night suffering the aching void; yet they expect the final reward of wrongdoing in the shape of a hard-earned sovereign! Not these the men for our money: rather those who appreciate the varied tastes and discrimination of their master's guests and "serve to palate," as the recipe books say. Not those who fluster you at dinner with a "champagne-sherry-or-red-'ock," but rather the kindly souls who whisper in your ear the quality or the vintage of the elixir they administer, and thus help you forward to the goal of every gastronome! The true butler, born as well as made, should supplement that scanty intelligence which is the endowment of too many hosts; he should differentiate between the quality and the fibre of his guests; he should divine that a parson's glass should always be filled to the brim, for that he can take a little more than other people, and yet be ill-satisfied. He should know, and many do, that Hermitage has the most religion, Hock the most sentiment, Champagne the most love, and Port the most charity; that Burgundy smiles, Hock winks, Champagne laughs, and Bordeaux puts a heart into all. He should know without telling that Madeira or Sherry should follow the soup, and further, that it will drink the softer if it has been uncorked some hours before. Haply he is cursed with an economical master, who will insist that wine left over to-night shall be drunk to-morrow. Now the butler will either drink it himself, as he should, or pour it down the sink, as it deserves; for "wine kept open all night is not worth a mite." Towards him a noble liberality should be extended: the more freedom you give him, the more zealously will he guard your interests against the plundering capacity of his underlings.

'Tis not so long ago that a feeble remonstrance was raised against one of the grandest butlers that ever died in a public-house: that there were never any cigars in the billiard-room by day. "Well, you see, sir," was his unanswerable answer, "some of my men smoke." Others there are who choose them men who profess teetotalism: this is to encourage hypocrisy at best, or rampant faddism at the worst. How shall a man serve the gift of the gods aright who abjures it in principle? He panders to a self-constituted crime, and he takes the edge off the flavour. And if he wears a blue ribbon on his coat and yet keeps the purple dawn upon his nose, how perilous your cellar! how subject to the gravest, because the pettiest, deceptions! Rather a butler who loves wine than one who actually or professedly dislikes it. Is it not better he should drink one bottle than give two away?

But it is part of a butler's lot that he should do other tasks worse than keep watch and guard over the cellar key, and pour out wine for alien drinkers. He is responsible for the plate, and, if in nothing besides, he shows herein the marked superiority of his sex, for if he do not apply the rouge himself, he constrains the footman or the page-boy. In no house where woman predominates do we ever find plate kept as plate should, darkly lustrous and beautifully bright. The trim cap and dainty apron of suburban Phyllis may please and delight some, but, for solid grandeur and substantial splendour, and, it may be added, potential enjoyment, we look solely to those houses whose threshold is guarded and whose portals are opened, by that great emblem of British respectability, the British Butler. Fair Phyllis may crown our brows with myrtle or with laurel, and there is always a plenty of laurel bushes where Phyllis lives, but it takes a man to crown our wine. To fill our glass with Lachryma Christi may wring a sympathetic tear from a woman's eye, but it was a master and not a mistress of arts, who, drinking liberally of this same wine, burst forth out of the abundance of his heart with the cry of

> "Utinam Christus vellet flere in patriâ nostrâ."

THE ENEMY

It was but a question of Time, on whose wings and amid whose plumes shelter all the woes and wonders of the world; it was but a question of Time, and now, at last, he has come. Borne along on soft, odorous winds from Xeres and Oporto, with the sunshine of Bordeaux in his eyes, and the vine leaves from the Côte d'Or in his hair, he has come, and, alas! he has come to stay. Redolent of all that is bright and cheerful in life, the scoff of our youth, the Cassandra of our prime, the scourge and the pest of our old age, he has laid his heavy hand upon our yet heavier boot. We are crucified with what Cicero called the dolours of the gout. The old brown sherry, only brought out at funerals and other rare festivals, but then indulged in copiously as the opportunity allowed, has found us out at last. For us his nuttiness, his richness, his dryness, are all mere abstract terms, *voces et preterea nihil*. No longer, charm he never so wisely with his choice selection of adjectives, those wondrously suggestive epithets of qualification and allurement, no longer dare we let his oily deliciousness gladden the palate of us upon whom Podagra has laid his dolorous finger. Henceforth life must be for us a stern fact, not to be laughed or quaffed away, but to be lived through and down and out. If we would seek for a moment to wander awhile into the shadowy rest-bringing bypaths of fancy and thought, or gallop impetuously into the very jousts of love and romance, into the tourney, as it were, of life, if we would watch the tossing, dancing bubbles in our champagne like stars of dawn luring us onward to a new youth, lo! in a moment this griping fiend has us writhing in his talons, and all becomes flat, jejune, unprofitable, stale. The long white fingers, tipped with the almond nails of perfect feature and complexion have grown, it seems to us, a trifle crooked, and there rises now and again an angry flush of ugly purple which irradiates them with an uncanny lurid glare from which we shrink, with a tiny shudder of inconsiderable horror, for we will not swell our own bogie man to unreasonable proportions. There appear, too, on the joints of those matchless fingers strange globosities, like the seeds which we were wont once to consider peculiar to the white currant, and if in our first flush of ignorance we would make question of our elders and wise-sayers as to what such things may be, get for an answer a contemptuous snort and ejaculatory monosyllables, "Pooh! Chalkstones! Gout! Port! Too much Port!" So, like Adam and Eve when they walked no longer in the beautiful nakedness of nescience, but bedecked themselves in the pants and continuations of acquired knowledge, we became ourselves one of the elders and wise-sayers, and gave up happiness with the acquisition of wisdom. Neither does this dread enemy of ours confine himself to joints and knuckles. His old name of Podagra is all too limited for the full scope of his power over the whole body. He will tolerate no sweet to make entrance into a system over which he exercises his tyrannous control, nor permit any acid, however refreshing, to keep harbour therein. What more poetical image in the world than to quaff the juice of the grape from Bordeaux vineyards and sun-bathed slopes of Epernay, and to dream we have clambered along the valleys and up the romantic ravines of snow-topped Helicon and tapped the fountains of Aganippe and Hippocrene, summoning the Muses themselves to play the Hebe for us? What lovelier labour does gastronomy know than to let its hand roam under the dark green strawberry leaves in English garden, and lure from its hiding-place the queen of fruits, as the rose of flowers, whether we take it cool and refreshing from the chilly shade, or hot and life-giving with the warmth of sun and heaven thick upon it? And yet—one single glass of claret, some half-dozen strawberries, and this monster will work his vengeance on us by making our blood tingle as though it had been sluiced with curry and ginger powder, and our bodies itch—strong evils claim a sturdy nomenclature—as though they had become the temporary camping-ground of the pestilence that walketh in darkness. The fiend is inexorable. Drink toast and water and he will leave us in peace, eat no fruit and taste no sugar, eschew butter and things which make for slipperiness, and he will go into temporary hiding; but he is there, for he has come, and he has come to stay. And on whom may we cast the blame? Surely not on ourselves, for we own not to the gallons we have drunken of wines heady and strong, wines tawny and fruity and loaded, wines creamy and nutty and rich, wines rosily opulent and aridly pale. We confess not to the pecks and bushels of fruits both fresh and preserved—no, we admit no impeachments soft or otherwise; we seek for scapegoats and a herd is at hand. Our fathers have eaten sour grapes and the teeth of the children are set on edge. The blame lies there, in parents and grandparents in whose veins coursed the nefarious sherry, the treacherous Madeira, the malignant port, the malicious hock, and the deceptive champagne. This is the one blessing with which Podagra tempers his many curses. He justifies our senses in blaming our thirsty progenitors for our own sufferings. Frailty, thy name is Heredity, and in thy name how many crimes have been committed? And yet, there was a hardiness in those forbears of ours which we cannot recall without admiration, though twitching toes and tingling blood check an exuberance of rapture. For they were mighty hunters and men of prowess in love and war, and we hear breathlessly of how, when they sat down to drink o' nights, they bolted the doors and divested them of their shoes and stockings before the wine went round; and as each bottle was finished they dashed it against the door, breaking it into a hundred fragments, so that none of them should make exit before, in the fulness of developed dawn, the servants came in and carried the recumbent forms with slow step and the measured rhythm of stertorous requiem to a more legitimate sleeping-place. Maybe these veteran topers, these *fontes et origines mali*, themselves grew old in years, and suffered their twinges, and swore their expostulatory swears; but they had drunk their fill; while we, a degenerate progeny, have no drink, and begin our twinges in our cradle, interrupting with our infantine oaths the lullaby of our nurses, and finding, as we grow older, our books in the pinching boots, sermons in chalkstones, and Gout in everything.

THE CONFESSION OF A WATER DRINKER

They tell me of our only Sarah that she keeps, or kept, in full evidence in her living-room the coffin which she predestinated as her ultimate abiding-place. Ascribe this act of innocuous bravado either to her innate youthfulness of disposition, or to her philosopher's contempt of death, and it shall pass for what it is worth. But it is with anything but a light heart, and with nothing of the philosopher in my nature that I find myself suddenly, in the twinkling of an eye, as it were, constrained to read—or write—my own burial service, or, at the least, to be present at my own interment. For it seems that that better part of me, that which I most loved and valued, has evanished from my life, so that I am now become a new thing. A degenerate regeneration has taken place, and a *novissimus homunculus* reigns in the stead of the old Noah. Only a sennight since, and I was even as that dear man in the story, who, led by his host through flower gardens, stables, picture galleries and museums, in mute and ear-less apathy, murmured at the end of his itinerary, in reply to his disappointed conductor, that he cared for nowt but drink. And now—now I have become a teetotaller; and the pity of it lies here, that I have become one not from conviction, but from constraint. For upon one of those nefarious days which come to most, and wreck not a few of us, it became a matter of necessity to insure that life so much enjoyed and loved, that life which in my own foolish way I had considered so emphat-ically "first-rate." But the raising of lucre was necessary, and in the train of necessity, with obvious insistence, came the insurance office. So it happened that I filled up a great white sheet with evasive answers to impertinent questions, and gave references to certain of my friends who,

I thought, would lie the firmest for me. But the worst was yet to be. For I was despatched to some wretched studio, or drug trap, near Grosvenor Square, to be examined by the consulting physician to the inquisition. And straightway he bade me strip mother-naked, and not Adam, nor yet Eve, felt the rigour of exposure more keenly than I in this parlour of the damned. And Aesculapius forced an ear-trumpet, which he called by another name, into my ribs, and pounded me with his rude fingers and aggressive thumbs. He hurt me, he bruised me, he insulted me, he probed me with questions as searching as a small-tooth comb, as debasing as the catechism itself. And then he bade me put on my discarded garments again, and, as he opened the door for my ignominious exit, conjured me, as I valued my life, to drink no more wine or strong drink. A week later I heard from the insurance company that my life being only a second-rate one a higher premium would be demanded. From that moment began suffering. For years back had I been an authority on all that in sunny climates and happy lands had been expressed from the grape. At every house where the cellar was renowned I had been received with open arms and bounteous glasses. The last bottle of the '47 port had gone down my throat of throats as a nation's darling is borne with solemn requiem to ancient abbey or historic cathedral. The mysteries of Bordeaux and Burgundian vintages had been my special delight. I had been found in the front rank at the gathering of the '89 champagnes. I had already girded my palatal loins for the crucial testing and sifting of the '93 clarets. My verdict had been sought expectantly and received respectfully. My *obiter dictum* that the old Madeira had sunk into his dotage and had become tart and peevish degraded him *instanter* into the second-class, so that he became the drink of those who were yet young and uninitiate. And now Death, on the pale horse Insurance, has bid me stand and deliver, and offers me life only on the degrading terms of abject teetotalism. All is over; no longer do I descend—oh! *facilis et amabilis descensus*—into the cellar and watch with silent joy the removal, for my own immediate delectation, of the "storied urn"; no longer does my "animated bust" glow with strange prospective and speculative yearnings. No more do I watch the solemn decantation which from a mere habit has risen into the dignity of a rite——a rite which has its acolytes as well as its high priest, who was none other than I. Vanished, alas! is that bittersweet anxiety of gaze lest the crust should be broken, the sediment too disturbed and thick.

Not now am I fitted to pronounce the verdict which had satisfied myself and host. Alas! *nuper idoneus vixi Lyaeo*! We——let the kindly plural shelter my singular aberration——we have become a degraded thing that has taken to drinking soda-water, or H_2O tempered with flavour of toast; our cup is filled, but only with misery and *aqua pura*, and yet——for a drinker's crown of sorrow is remembering wetter days——an ironclad of the first class had floated in the champagne we have drank in the past. As we write, the 1893 vintage of claret is coming on. It is to be the best vintage since 1875. We had been careful to secure a lease in perpetuity at a peppercorn rent of a great empty cellar free from vibration and all disturbance. This it was our glorious intention to fill from ground to rafter (our shirts having been all pawned) with the splendid promises which Margaux utters and Lafite re-echoes. Of what avails it now? We have taken the vine leaves from out of our hair and our second-rate life refuses to be comforted. The soda-water spits its little puny, restless, damnable bubbles against the cold white glass of a degenerate child of Bacchus, a glass which once had glowed and gleamed with alternate ruby and amber gold. Of what avails all our learning now? What boots it that we have learned to love, if death, in the guise of an insurance company's doctor, has robbed us of our beloved? Take us—no, me—up tenderly, treat me with care. Bring out your grocer's Marsala, your cheapest Gilbey sherry (his dearest is as good as you may drink). Palm off upon us your second-day claret, your corked port, your dotaged Madeira. It is all one to us. Good wine and bad wine are alike now. It is all sour, all bad. "D— you, waiter; why can't you bring us that Salutaris water?" To compose an epitaph on our own dead self is impossible. We can but adopt that of another who died, like ourselves, of a broken heart: "Here lies one whose name was writ in soda-water."

PUSHKIN PRESS—THE LONDON LIBRARY

"FOUND ON THE SHELVES"

THE LONDON LIBRARY (a registered charity) is one of the UK's leading literary institutions and a favourite haunt of authors, researchers and keen readers.

Membership is open to all.

Join at www.londonlibrary.co.uk.

www.pushkinpress.com